Daught

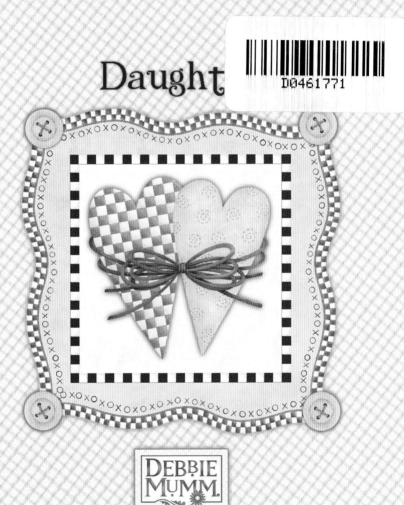

Debbie Mumm.

www.debbiemumm.com

new seasons™

Daughters come in every
shape and size,
but each fits perfectly
into her mother's heart.

When you bring a daughter into
the world, you imagine the
woman she can be,
and you can't help but
reexamine the woman you are.

I hope two things for you:
that you are grounded,
and that you
have wings.

As the world changes, one
thing will stay the same:
You'll always be my little girl.

My hope is that the decisions
I make today will help you
to make the right
choices tomorrow.

Dear daughter, may you have a
long, happy life filled with
wonder, achievement, and love.

When you were born, I thought about all the things I needed to teach you. I didn't realize I'd learn from you every bit as much as you'd learn from me.

I love you simply because
you're you.

The birth of a daughter
is a small, quiet miracle.

I never knew what beauty was
till the moment I first saw
my daughter's face.

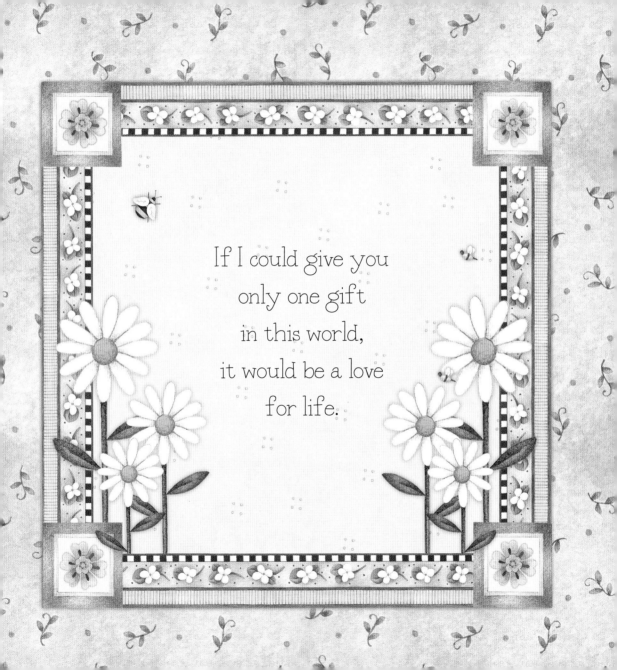

If I could give you
only one gift
in this world,
it would be a love
for life.

Daughter, I will always be
there for you. When your
heart breaks, I will do
everything I can to mend it.
When you face difficulties,
I will help you triumph over them.

When you find joy and
success, I will dance with
you in celebration
and sing your praises
to everyone I see.

A daughter's smile fills the
room with light.
A daughter's laugh fills the
world with music.

I've accomplished many
things in my life,
but having a daughter is the
best thing I've ever done.

A daughter's love
brings sunshine to her
family's garden.

Daughter, you may be too big
now to hold on my lap,
but I will always hold you
in my heart.

One glimpse of my daughter's funny little smile, or her sweet, crinkled nose, and my heart is filled with more love than I ever thought it could bear.

Dear daughter, may you have the courage to go after the things you want, and the perseverance to keep working till you get them.

A daughter is proof
that angels exist.

I look at my daughter in amazement. She is so much a part of me, yet she is completely a woman of her own.

People often talk of the
sacrifices a mother makes for
her children, but everything
given is received back tenfold.

Daughter, the greatest gift
you can give to the world is for
you to be yourself.

A mother's idea of perfect
beauty is the way her
daughter's fingers curl around
her cheek as she sleeps.

Motherhood involves a
spectrum of emotions:
fear, excitement, guilt, and pride.
But above all, there is sheer joy.

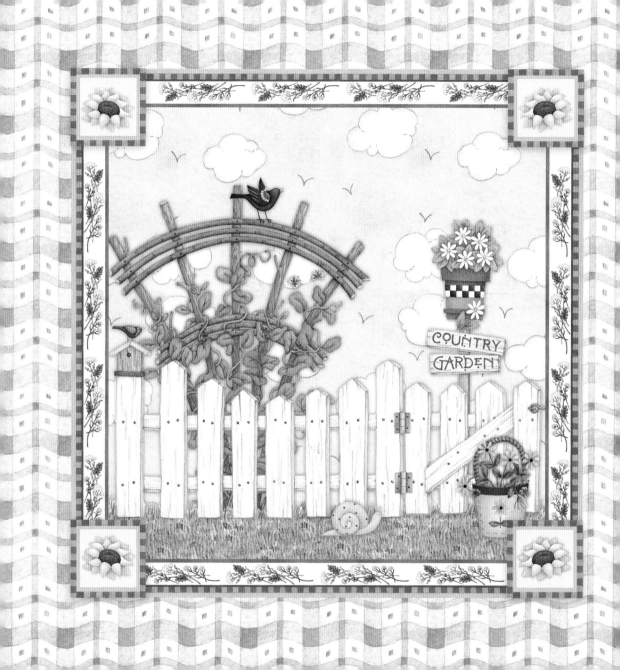

COUNTRY
GARDEN

The world becomes new every day when I look at it through the eyes of my daughter.

My daughter forms close attachments: When she was a baby, it was to her grandfather. When she was a little girl, it was to her nursery school teacher. And now that she's a teenager, it's to the phone!

I never dreamed the day would come when the little girl who loved to play dollhouse would finally get a place of her own.

Being a mother has made me a
better person. I now try harder
than ever to do what is
right because I know
my daughter is watching.

There is only one pretty
child in the world, and
every mother has it.

-CHINESE PROVERB-

When the world closes in,
there's nothing so comforting as
the voice on the other end of the
line saying, "Hi honey, it's Mom."

Having a daughter fills every
moment of my life with grace.

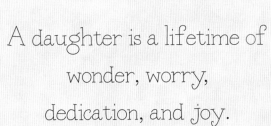

A daughter is a lifetime of
wonder, worry,
dedication, and joy.

When life gets hard, and every day seems to bring another obstacle, one glimpse of my daughter's sweet face reminds me that no matter what I must do, it's worth it.

Good daughters
make good mothers.

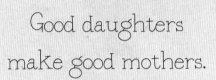

-ABIGAIL G. WHITTLESEY-

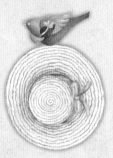

Fancy clothes, ice cream,
and a walk in the park
were the recipe
for a perfect day
when you were young.
Not much has changed!

It is from our daughters
that we learn the virtues of
kindness and gentleness.

Daughters are the joyful
memories of the past,
the happy moments of the
present, and the hope and
promise of the future.

Sometimes the best thing a
parent can do is to remember
what it was like to be a child.

What the daughter does,
the mother did.

–JEWISH PROVERB–

RED Radishes

When you were little,
I realized there was
a great big world out there
you didn't know about.
My job was to ready you for
the discovery.

When your daughter goes out
into the world, a little piece of
you goes with her.

Raising a daughter can be a
joy, a challenge, a delight,
and sometimes a trial.
But most of all, it is a privilege.

A lovely girl is
above all rank.

-CHARLES BUXTON-

Children never turn out
exactly the way you'd hoped;
they turn out better in a
thousand amazing ways.

Daughters, like roses,
are each beautiful
and perfect
in their own way.